reflections

Praise for the book

Kapil Sibal's deep poetic flair is an unexpected talent. In *Reflections*, he gives us, in flowing rhyme, a bird's-eye view of what he has encountered in life, and he has seen more of life than many of us have. In delightful and gently acerbic verse, he has given us the benefit of a life's experience.

—Keki N. Daruwalla
Renowned poet and novelist

Kapil's continuing creativity and literary ability is quite amazing. In his latest book *Reflections*, the poems cover a spectrum of moods—politics, love and introspection—all presented poetically.

—Dr Karan Singh
Statesman, educationalist,
philanthropist, author and poet

These excursions in verse reveal Kapil Sibal's innermost concerns, his political preoccupations, his heartfelt emotions and his sense of mischief. An enjoyable read.

—Dr Shashi Tharoor
Acclaimed writer and Member of Parliament, Lok Sabha

reflections
in rhyme and rhythm

KAPIL SIBAL

RUPA

Published by
Rupa Publications India Pvt. Ltd 2022
7/16, Ansari Road, Daryaganj
New Delhi 110002

Sales centres:
Allahabad Bengaluru Chennai
Hyderabad Jaipur Kathmandu
Kolkata Mumbai

Copyright © Kapil Sibal 2022

This is a work of fiction. Names, characters, places and incidents are either the product of the author's imagination or are used fictitiously and any resemblance to any actual person, living or dead, events or locales is entirely coincidental.

All rights reserved.

No part of this publication may be reproduced, transmitted, or stored in a retrieval system, in any form or by any means, electronic, mechanical, photocopying, recording or otherwise, without the prior permission of the publisher.

ISBN: 978-93-5520-235-2

First impression 2022

10 9 8 7 6 5 4 3 2 1

The moral right of the author has been asserted.

Printed in India

This book is sold subject to the condition that it shall not, by way of trade or otherwise, be lent, resold, hired out, or otherwise circulated, without the publisher's prior consent, in any form of binding or cover other than that in which it is published.

*To all those whose words weave
the magic that eludes prose*

Contents

Critics Must Pause	1
Muse	3

Section–1
Politics of Introspection

The Charade	7
Miscalculation	12
Courage	16
The Untold Story	18
Falling from Grace	20
Need Handymen	22
Unicorns	24
The Gullible	27
Yelp and Rally	29
Robbing-Hood	30
Time to Smile	31
Zero Tolerance	32
Out of Sight	33
Facebook's Faceless	34
Walk the Talk	35
Vote-Bank Politics	37
Hypocrisy	38
The Lies That Sell	41

Section–2
The Storms Ahead

Big Brother	45
Battles to Fight	46
Fuelling Hatred	48
Change	50
Full Circle	52
Self-incrimination	54
Misinformation	57
Love of Liberty	59
Yearning for Truth	61
Hope	64
Empathy	66

Section–3
The Search for Truth

The Story of Human Plight	71
As Lies Unfold	73
The March of Civilization	75
Evolution	80
Commercial Cruise	81
Rudderless	84
Remember	86
Despair and Hope	88
Marvel of Nature	90
Privacy	92
Destiny	94
Breaching Norms	96
Unchained	98
Internet	100

Looking Ahead	101
The Joy of Being	102
Marching On	105
Betrayed	107
Sumptuous	112
Bored Lives	113

Section–4
Love—The Elixir for All Seasons

Discover	119
Evergreen	121
The Rising Tide	122
At Ease	124
Destined	126
Missing You	127
Remembering	129
Caring	131
Ageing	133
Understanding	134
Only We Matter	135
Discretion	136
References	137

Critics Must Pause

Was delighted that
you spared some time
to review my book
in broken rhyme

Reviews in rhyme
scant analysis
symptom of mental
paralysis

Rhyme and rhythm
not meant for those
suffering from literary
comatose

Some culture vultures
have little taste,
do literary reviews
with undue haste

Rhyme like prose
we must savour
enjoy its texture
poetic flavour

Gulping it down
without much ado
lose out on taste and
a sensible review

Muse

You inspired me
to etch my thoughts
as they unfold
in rhyme

Helped me to bare
my heart and soul
for years in
quarantine

Section-1

Politics of Introspection

The Charade

Distrust all those
who are in power
leitmotif
of Anna's war

Jan Lokpal is
the way to go
you are 'corrupt'
if you say 'no'

His stir will be
non-violent
along the way
brook no dissent

Gandhian ways
of his own brand
us mortals fail
to understand

Morals espoused
benchmarks for you
transgressors be
whipped black and blue

In Ralegaon
those who dare drink
tie them to poles
and help them think[1]

Four musketeers
have led the way
they are cash rich
and here to stay

Saw thousands throng
to hear him say
no matter what
he'll have his way

Donations made
helped them secure
the centre stage
for an encore

Perhaps it was
the RSS
paving the way
for their success[2]

Through Anna they
might sell a dream
benefit those
behind the scenes

Mesmerize
the laity
destabilize
our polity

Media will seize
moments like these
build and increase
its TRPs

Call it free speech
allege, abuse
riding on a
commercial cruise

Help build discord
disdain, dissent
breed mistrust of
establishment

The focus of
the camera's eye
allows no space
to question why

Our world narrows
down to a spot
that image helps
the truth to rot
The medium is
to blame for this
helps us believe
all is amiss

Musketeers were
on their own trip
made Anna lose
his vice-like grip

Disclosures made
seemed to suggest
moral frailty
with no regrets

The pulpiteers
who once held sway
with time exposed
their feet of clay

Anna too lost
his moral high
with glucose he
had on the sly[3]

One slap for him
was not enough
he wanted two
but was rebuffed

His politics
too has a slant
biased postures
came home to haunt

This tortuous lap
made us look weak
our future then
sounded most bleak

Our sprint ahead
was cut to size
some truths hit home
so did some lies

Miscalculation

Intrigued, my friend
wished to discuss
the CAG's
concept of 'loss'

What is 2G
he asked to know
'a spectrum that
will always flow
a highway that
will never freeze
through snowstorms and
tumultuous seas'
explained it was
a scarce resource
his thoughtful mind
was set on course

Band of airwaves
shrinks distances
talk to loved ones
in times amiss

reaching out to
those in distress
give hope when lives
are in a mess
such benefits
will only flow
if we can keep
our tariffs low

That way both you
and I will gain
yet 'loss' is the
constant refrain

To calculate
the loss, we must
assess the gain
and then adjust
you can't compute
in money terms
the value of
hidden returns
connect people
in ways unheard
presumptive gains
to be factored
this was not done

as we all know
that's part of it
there's more to go

The treasury too
had got its share
through aggregates
telcos declared
profits increased
as customers grew
the government too
received its dues

This fuss about
presumptive loss
tossed numbers with
a maverick's gloss

It's not about
losses or gains
we fear our folks
now with disdain
will doubt what we
indeed achieved
and charge us with
corruption, greed

The nation too
might lose its sheen
economic growth
its pace and steam

To the CAG
I wish to say
history will prove
you wrong one day

Courage

Time to reflect
what we
have gained
left lives and
institutions
maimed

As students
held protests
in vain
your treatment
evidenced
disdain

The lathi blows
the gunshot
wounds
the broken
panes in
barged-in rooms

You broke
their backs
their spirits not
these torchbearers
will stem
the rot

Your diktats
thrust through
violent means
attempts
to subjugate
demean

Will tear
asunder
what we built
take note
our spirit
will not wilt

You'll come
and go
forgotten soon
came as a
harbinger
of doom

The Untold Story

The saga of Rafale
is yet to be known
the campaign acerbic
in substance and tone

The G-to-G contract
a smokescreen for some
but papers will reveal how
the foul deed was done

The offset bonanza
was layered with cream
our Shouries and Bhushans
made Rafale lose steam[4]

Dassault of French vintage
co-opted with ease
claiming Court's clean chit
proved absence of sleaze

HAL found it was short-changed
for no fault of theirs
our upright Parrikar
was caught unawares

But clueless Sushmaji
was twiddling her thumbs
South Block too felt left out
they fed it with crumbs

Post-facto decisions
with some legalese
weapons to distinguish
between chalk and cheese

Unsettled these matters
will trouble our minds
the truth till now hidden
will surface with time

Despite allegations
the Rafale will fly
what you say matters not
a lie is a lie

Falling from Grace

It's betrayal
with expectations
shattered
as I open my eyes
to witness
the fall
of an edifice
that protected me
in the comfort
of which I
cherished hope

Why would I
fight for those
who let us down?

Will have to
fight them now

Brick by brick
those who dreamt
for us

lie still within
the ashes of
Eternity
leaving us
to run
with the baton

It is their
betrayal that
makes me pick up
the remains of
broken oaths
and hold them
together
for us

Need Handymen

The judge
of causes
a dying breed

Mindsets
have changed
I must concede

The poor
have no
access to court

How do they
pierce
the rich man's fort

When will
the common man
believe

His wounds
for years
will one day heal

The wheels
of justice
slowly grind

Contours
of justice
ill-defined

To lose faith
is with
danger fraught

One wonders
who will
stem the rot

Essence
of justice
is fair play

Escapes
the powerless
today

Latch on
to hope
live in despair

The system
needs
urgent repair

Unicorns

Not easy
to define
the truth
that may be
yours
not mine

And yet
you push it
down
my throat
invoking
the divine

Often the
contours of
my truth
I know
not why
they change

Your static
mindset
makes
me feel
I am the one
to blame

My thoughts
perceptions
change
evolve
discover
I was wrong

I try
to understand
why your
convictions
are
so strong

I feel
a misfit
in your midst
an alien
out of
tune

in time
I hope
you might
believe
opinions are
a boon

For in my
thoughts
another point
of view
perhaps
resides

One day
you might
just realize
your truth
was
calcified

The Gullible

Am part of
the debris
as the footsteps
of today
move on

I was the one
who built
the forgotten
whitewashed
yesteryears

Irreverence
targets those
who think
not of today
but laud the past

Yet upon
the shoulders
of the past
is seen
what lies ahead

He conquered
minds who
knew not
those bygone years
but lived in fear

The aridity
of their despair
helped him
sell them
grasslands

He too
will be lost
in the unsung
pages
of history

Yet
another
sorcerer
will manipulate
thirsty minds

Yelp and Rally

The Rafale I bought off the shelf
know not why Congress now 'yelp'
did business with ease
with my expertise
with Hollande then willing to help

The Rafale is right up my alley
will ride in the cockpit with Sally
impressed with manoeuvres
with shakers and movers
'Republic' will join in the rally

Robbing-Hood

Never forget to remember
that fateful day in November
at the stroke of midnight
with a surgical strike
all have-nots made to surrender

all that they had earned in their lives
including the savings of wives
were frozen and worthless
the rich were not cashless
it was easy for them to survive

Time to Smile

Woke up with a start when I hit
250 while in the cockpit
I counted the number
when deep in my slumber
the truth will be told bit by bit

Zero Tolerance

This terror strike
won't make us fall
will stand together
take a call

The precious lives
of brave hearts lost
befitting must
be our riposte

Blinded are minds
where demons breed
strike hard to make
them grieve and bleed

Out of Sight

Our
farmers are
in deep
distress

No
Zuckerberg
can clear
this mess

Attend
to them
look to
their needs

Do not
ignore
the hand
that feeds

Facebook's Faceless

As farmers die
Modi flies high
a selfie splurge
with Zuckerberg
stop at the Bay
far, far away
from millions who
voted for you
deliver on
your promises
if not meet with
your nemeses

Walk the Talk

How often
have you
heard us say

It's time
to introspect

Angered
by this
constant refrain

By promises
unkept

Reach out
to those
who matter most

To understand
their pain

Silently
must
work for them

They'll vote
for you again

Articulate
what
you believe

Fear not
what others say

Let's
walk along
the truthful path

The sun
will rise some day

Vote-Bank Politics

Cannot allow
cadres to read
we'll have to then
often concede
they are literate
and we are not
and they will make
our system rot
making them slaves
to their own thought

Literates if party
cadres fill
they'll march ahead
while we stand still
open thought is
anathema
we believe in
our own karma

We'll always be
what now we are
that's why we do
not travel far

Hypocrisy

It's time for us
to be austere
the message is
that we too care

We must shed
weight, economize
all budgets must
be cut to size

Impose a ban
on eating rice
conveys a sense
of sacrifice

Then you will know
how farmers feel
the time has come
to eat one meal

Must learn to starve
as others do
and feel the pinch
of the other shoe

Our policies
will make no sense
our motto now
is 'abstinence'

Be Spartan in
your thoughts and ways
while India goes
through real tough days

In offices
stop use of lifts
another way
to practise thrift

Those who sign files
without a care
not bother with
what's written there

For them, at work
Put off the lights
we must save power
with budgets tight

That way perhaps
we'll understand
the problems of
the common man

How often have
we shed a tear
for those who live
in constant fear

As death shadows
their daily lives
and suicides
are no surprise

And as we deal
with sleepless nights
discomfort of
cross-country flights

The farmer then
will think we share
his suffering, for
we really care

Flagellation
is at its best
with abstinence
and all the rest

Self-denial
will give us hope
as we continue
with this soap

The Lies That Sell

Desilt your mind
to help us see
how you conserve
your energy

Your solar cells
process modules
make us all feel
like utter fools

Your heady words
through empty space
emerge with such
innocuous grace

The Equator's warmth
emboldens you
dense thoughts somehow
through you ring true

Your urbane ways
make us believe
our lost world, we
must soon retrieve

Bring you back home
at any cost
will treasure that,
we have, since lost

The vision of
your long-term plans
will enthuse your
despondent fans

Help us wade through
our darkest days
like Moses, wave
to show the way

Your thoughtful words
will see us sink
till then you'll walk
us to the brink

At NDC your speech unread
your lullaby a watershed

Section-2

The Storms Ahead

Big Brother

The new God
technology
watches me
wade through
each moment
of my life

Stripping me
of my
comfort zone
where I and
my God alone
were privy to

But this God
is intrusive
unforgiving

Battles to Fight

Love
has no taint
yet it is
flagged

Why then
my Allah's
always
dragged

Between us
spaces
shrunk
with time

The doubts
we had
were
left behind

Oblivious
of the
storms
ahead

Of demons
who might
leave us
dead

Will they
succeed
to break
our faith

They will
molest
our love
with hate

Till when
will we
escape
their wrath

When they
catch up
all will
be lost

Fuelling Hatred

I challenge you
to a duel
of words
ready to
excoriate
your being
for the venom
with which
I throw them
at you
constantly
to evoke
unease and
discomfort
will make you
either
run away
or in anger
open up
a fault line
I will
latch on to

My
daily appetite
is fuelled
by my
abusive
routine
in which
my lies
about you
germinate
and multiply
so others
can believe
that which
is not true

Change

Our laws
are not
in heaven
made

May suffer
hell
if not
obeyed

Laws
are norms
beliefs
sustained

Once thought
that they
were
God-ordained

Weapons
through which
our minds
are tamed

And seeds
of change
remain
contained

The victims
of
our laws
oft see

Chinks
in our
laws,
armouries

Within those
whom
the law
ensnares

Be sure
the seeds
of change
are there

Full Circle

Take two
steps up
and two steps
down

What
moves away
oft comes
around

In
freedom too
somehow
feel bound

To you
and this
and that

Can't change
the seasons
of my life

The contours
of a
sharpened
knife

Excoriates
my layered
strife

Makes us
reflect
and sad

Lush
green fields
and desert sands

Both coexist
go hand
in hand

Yet time
unravels
what we planned

The good
comes with
the bad

Self-incrimination

You picked
me up

Disgorged
my very
being

Ate up
all the

Marrow
from my

Bones
and
left me

Hollow
unhinged

Lost
my bearings

And
myself
in

Your
vile
embrace

Where
contours
of

Good
and evil

Are
frayed
and I

A
broken
horse

In
confinement

Do
your
bidding

Accuse
myself

Excoriate
my being
with a knife

Misinformation

Ignorance
is a state
of bliss

For all
of us
an oasis

Of arrogance
in which
we thrive

Vilifying with
jaundiced
eyes

Contra
views
be cut to size

With
prejudice
thus on the rise

Those
out of line
must ostracize

To be
the target
of our lies

Love of Liberty

Armed with
the courage
of my thoughts
I plough
a lonely furrow

A cacophony
of sounds
nibbling at my
sensibilities

Like termites
eat into
the vitals of
my few beliefs

I must hold on
for that alone
helps sustain
my sanity

Liberty is
a torch
kept aflame
by the fuel
of deeds

Ploughing
lonely
furrows
where
freedom breeds

Yearning for Truth

I looked
and saw
naked
and raw

Nature
in bloom
without
a flaw

Within it
searched
for the
truth

Bare
as it lay
both rough
and smooth

No dressing
seen
nothing
to hide
no veil
of secrecy
inside

No special
love
no cast
aside

No need
to take you
for a
ride

Yearn
for the stark
and open
world

Where
stories
don't have
to be told

Truth
oft
slips away
unseen

You never
know
what could
have been

Hope

In solitude
measure
my life

With a
dustbin
by my side

Journey
a transient
interlude

Under
our murky
open skies

Ugly faces
of pelf
and loot

Immersed
under a
slew of lies

Crumpled
the dreams
I woke up with

And promises
I hoped
to ride

Yet I
feel that
all is not lost

Those
after me
are sure to glide

Keeping
a watchful
eye on all

Those
homo sapiens
tsetse flies

Empathy

Let's see
the world
through
other's eyes

Hold close
console
when someone
cries

To
understand
the pain
they feel

With time
we know
their wounds
will heal

They too
must feel
that they belong

Targets of
monumental
wrongs

That might
just help them
to forget

And hope
that others
might regret

Make them stand
walk ahead
with grace

Convince
them that
they have a place

Where they can
breathe
feel free to speak

Knowing
they have the
right to seek

Justice
by those who
will decide

Find out
why they
were vilified

That might just
help them
sleep with ease

And bring
the unjust
to their knees

Justice will
help thus
keep afloat

All that
they have
is only hope

Section-3

The Search for Truth

The Story of Human Plight

Hope ends
in despair

Gives birth
to hope
as we go
down the
slippery slope

Crave to
conquer
lost empires
the edifice of
our desires
Seek crutches
to face tomorrow
success eludes
followed by
sorrow
In our defeats
succumb

to nature's might
story of
the human plight

As Lies Unfold

The camera views
with just one eye
I wish it could
have two
along with it
a mind that helps
to find out what
is true

The truth is not
frozen in time
with images
we see
those peddling it
as lies unfold
bruising its sanctity

It's just one way
to look at things
see them as we

perceive
are harbingers of
prejudice
meant only to deceive

With my two eyes
absorb all sights
beyond them search
for more
the truth perhaps
eludes me oft
afraid to be
too sure

I have struggled
within myself
to find out what
is true
constrained to tell
the moving screen
cannot believe
in you

The March of Civilization

We thoughtfully use
our forks and knives
talk of scandals
surrounding lives
of kings and queens
of yesteryears
who reigned to kill
and shed no tears
the trophies of
barbaric wars
were kingdoms won
with wounds and scars
survival was
a daily tryst
true loyalty
a virtue missed
quest to conquer
a central theme
that underlies
us mortals' dreams
Palace intrigues
empires lost

aggrandizement
but at what cost?
how else would then
kingdoms survive?
not go to war
would be naive
men were fodder
in battlefields
triumphs brought home
increasing yields
wars sources of
riches and wealth
these helped enhance
the kingdom's health
victories perceived
as acts divine
wars commerce of
medieval times

Science triumphed
discoveries made
new riches sought
by pushing trade
then came engines
with steam to roll
commerce in goods
grew manifold

enslaved humans
like chattels dealt
empires grew
so did their wealth
swiftly transformed
economies
the source of wealth
were colonies
stripped them bare
transferred their wealth
with open loot
if not by stealth

The concept of
the nation state
made empires
seem out of date
the struggles for
freedom were stoked
by glorious deeds
of simple folk
the unnamed who
gave up their lives
merged with the crowd
who swore to strive
the swelling mass
sea of protest

burst forth with hope
for fresh conquests
broke free to see
the midnight sun
lit up the sky
freedom was won

Yet history oft
repeats itself
through lust, deceit
conquests and pelf
the means perhaps
are now unique
insiders trade
corporate intrigue
seek victories
through IPR's
multinationals
contemporary Czars
hackers will use
our cyberspace
will launch attacks
without a trace
control markets
seek dominance
the surest way
to influence

new wave conquests
fresh battlefields
behind it all
is human greed

Evolution

Lava of words
emotive
outbursts of
unreflecting
minds

Voices unheard
have come alive
new-found freedom
unchartered
blind

Virgin spaces
ask questions why
the way looks
porcupined

Seen struggles
through centuries
as solutions
emerge with
time.

Commercial Cruise

Celluloid flows
impact the mind
weave messy tales
raw, unrefined
seeking answers
in real time

The truth often
fails to emerge
the message though
is to help purge
the guilty through
a visual splurge

Immobilized
our victims lie
as vultures wait
for them to die
their appetites
are in full cry

Alive they feed
and savour pain
these trophies earn
public acclaim
their targets have
been put to shame

The truth, alas,
is cast aside
the printed word
now seldom guides
the visual form
is what decides

The fourth estate
is now the first
it seeks to quench
consumers' thirst
seek cesspools of
all forms of lust

All news is now
only bad news
there is no space
for other views
no valiant tales
to help enthuse

Our nation's youth
who dare to dream
gallop, despite
the moving screen
discover worlds
not so far seen

The time has come
to introspect
to trust rather
than to suspect
be sceptical
to help reflect

The printed word
will save the day
help understand
all shades of grey
help traffic move
the other way

Make sure discourse
is civilized
our breaking news
be not contrived
have its content
democratized

Rudderless

I still remember
our darkest night
as we witnessed
the flow of
moving lights
while the last
flicker of
a precious life
left us
orphaned

Without
her anchor
breathless
and unfree
groped for
crutches in
the silent abyss
of uncertainty
not knowing
where to begin

Collected
with care
the tattered remains
of our memories
weaving them
within
the recesses
of our minds
as we all
felt forlorn

Remember

What is it
about my life
that I
must not
forget

Hands
guiding
the little steps
to make me
walk ahead

Those who
helped me
script the words
as they escaped
my mind

Guided me
through thick
and thin
without a word
unkind

When in gloom
they lit
the sky
with fireworks
and more

In happy times
shared
in my joy
that helped
me dig for more

And as they
watch me
from far
I wish they
somehow know

Embrace
those moments
close to heart
as I get up
to go

Despair and Hope

I stared
at her face
bereft of
emotion

Her glazed
eyes
betrayed
her abject
surrender

Even
the spectre
of hope
eluded her

While
my eyes
absorbed
with ease
and ecstasy

The
opportunities
at my
doorstep

Armed with
all the tools
to help me
conquer

Yet
my victories
provide
no solace

For in her
defeat
I feel that I
have let
her down

Marvel of Nature

My thoughts
meander
like the mist

Silently
with ease

Caressing
leaflets
of my life

Swaying
with the breeze

Through
forest slopes
and mountain tops

Gorges
and ravines

Seeking
solace
with yearnings for

Yet
another dream

The mist
clears up
stark nature stares

Find myself
at peace

I am a child
of what
I see

Nature's
mysteries

Privacy

Many a
world
is found
within

Beneath
the texture
of my
skin

Stories
untold
in mortal
frames

Will die
with me
and my
remains

I show
the world
my mask
not me

Suppress
the truth
most
willingly

The
real me
with tales
untold

Will
vanish
with me
in the cold

Destiny

Wrapped
in the
luxury

Of my
cushioned
life

I sleep

While
millions
seek

The
sunlight
in their lives

And weep

Tomorrow
brings
hope

As new
worlds
open up

For me

While
others
search

Seek
answers
of their

Destiny

Breaching Norms

Let's
breach
those norms
we often find

Must
liberate
our love
confined

To lose
ourselves
in moments
blind

Searching
for
pastures
undefined

Release
our bodies
from our
mind

Leave
what is
manicured,
refined

Unchained

It's
habit

That
dulls
my brain

As it
chugs
along

The
beaten
track

And yet
the
threat
of change

Unnerves
me

For it
disturbs

The
comfort
and
routine
of certainty

I
desire
to be
unbound

Buffeted
by gusty
winds

Grappling
with the
vicissitudes
of fortune
to stay alive

Internet

A myriad
words
without
a face

Oceans
of data
commonplace

A springboard
ready
to disgrace

As it
moves on
without
a trace

And yet
I wish to
share
this space
With
you

Looking Ahead

When things
have run their
course

Walk away
with no
remorse

The Joy of Being

To live
and to be
alive

To decay
or to
thrive

The
measured
moments
of my life

Are tiresome

Predictable

Like my
migraine
which
pounds me
without
remorse

I succumb

Knowing
that it will
return
to haunt
me

A
blessed
moment

A
wet
kiss

A brush
with innocence

The sunset
of a
receding
wave

Moments
of wilderness
in the

womb of
nature

A surge
of joy
within

My mind
sprints

To
nowhere
land

With a
smile

Marching On

The tremors of
uncertainty
engulf me
as I sip
cups of tea
and slip
into my shoes
every morning

The world
around me
is sugarless

The
sweeteners
being
cancerous

My shoes
hurt
as I walk

Egging me

To slip into
someone
else's
empty shoes

There is
a vacuum
to be filled

Mine too

As night falls

Betrayed

I never
knew
that you
would
walk away

I thought
that you
would
always be

In times
of need
right next
to me

I never
thought
that I
would see
this day

I never
knew
that you
would
walk away

I never
knew
that you
would
let me
down

I trusted
you
I leaned
on you

Savoured
the time
I spent
with you

I never
thought
that you

would
run me
down

I never
knew
that you
would
let me
down

I never
thought
that I
would see
this day

You
left me
right
out in
the cold

I
wondered
why

I was
not told

Guess
you never
thought
what you
would say

I never
thought
that I
would see
this day

Now that
I think
you
always
had your
say

You
never cared
how I
had felt

Just
one more
prize
under
your belt

Look
around
for yet
another
prey
I never
thought
that I
would see
this day

I never
knew
that you
would
walk away

Sumptuous

Dear Fatsy please
don't disappear
urge you to be
substantially there

Don't fade away
before our eyes
your presence we
seek otherwise

For if you starve
reduce your girth
you'll have to shed
some kilo's worth

Happiness comes
along with gain
precious assets
must be maintained

Bored Lives

Boring mindsets
conventional,
most often, one
dimensional

Look not beyond
their nose to see
life in its full
diversity

A wife, a home
a comfort zone
a garden where
roses are grown

A bank account
fattens with time
socks, matching shoes
that always shine

All meals on time
health foods consume
landscape must not
be out of tune

Hush puppies and
with dogs on leash
shelf, classic works
like *War and Peace*

At home, nothing
is out of place
the object arts
add to the grace

Crackers and cheese
with fruity wine
summer cruise down
the river Rhine

Nine holes at golf
weekend routine
cut business deals
at pastures green

For those who have
lived life this way
unmindful of
Judgment Day

You'll know that you
prospered and thrived
but missed out on
being alive

Section-4

Love—The Elixir for All Seasons

Discover

You, the Fagun
that I await
though I believe
a little late

This spring will last
for years to come
and make you feel
like twenty-one

Tender thoughts
tuck them away
do nurture them
in your own way

As we relearn
our youthful ways
our past will feel
like distant days

Our instincts then
will spring alive
to fertilize
moments that thrive

Hyphenated
provide the link
seek ecstasy
no time to think

Evergreen

I carry your
fragrance with me
as you overwhelm me
while you are adrift
in the eternal world
of silence
as I recede
you resurrect
help me inhale with ease
knowing that the lapse
of time will take care of
our distance
I know not why
this love endures
for you left me no choice
as I look to find
the elixir for
all seasons

The Rising Tide

Within my mind
you oft reside
I want you close
right by my side
find new ways to
expand our space
find freedom in
a warm embrace
don't tell me then
you wanted this
just one more time
another kiss
seek moments when
all else recedes
just you and me
with our felt need
we cast aside
our sense of time
wish to be yours
while you are mine
not think, just feel
absorb, explore

as cushioned waves
bring us ashore
will seek refuge
under your skin
help us to quell
the storm within

At Ease

The purest form
of love is its
silhouette

Intangible
and attached to me
Otherwise, your
touch makes me
respond to
my senses
within me
silently

I want to love
without my lips
feeling your
breathless ways
wandering
aimlessly

The comfort of
your silhouette
fulfills me
exploring
terrains
leisurely

Destined

I never knew
it would be you
I never thought
you'd say 'why not'
the door ajar
sought sites afar
explored with ease
to seek our peace
let moments melt
with moves un-spelt
us two alone
to sigh and moan
afloat in time
relived our prime
in silence spoke
afresh with hope
lost worlds regained
with love ordained
no going back
no changing track

Then felt I knew
it would be you

Missing You

My constant
soulmate
is a
gadget
without a voice

Isolates,
helps me
wade through
alleyways
of my choice

Far away
from
public gaze
I savour
what I see

Yet I miss
those
fingertips
to play around
with me

Exploring
through apps
and more
you're closer
to me now

How I wish
to hold
you tight
and kiss your
furrowed brow

Remembering

Time flies
but memories
stay fresh
with timeless
ease
seeding the
wasteland of
ennui that
engulfs
the monotony
of time itself

Evergreen
without the
weight of
age
you step
ahead with
me
waiting with
bated breath

those moments
of freedom

Within
together

Caring

Take me
beyond
my dreams
to worlds
woven in
wilderness

Relentless
storms
that rise
within,
simmer
with a caress

My fingertips
will trace
our being
my lips
will do the
rest

Share
poetic
wayward
thoughts
in solitude
that's blessed

To have
each other
in this way
no whiff
of a
conquest

The rhythmic
sonnet
of our lives
gives
comfort
to our nest

Ageing

Your love
has aged,
matured

Its vintage
has with
time
endured

Understanding

I wear
my anger
on my sleeve

Throw
it away
when I receive

Your love
in constant
lava flows

Sears
my being
and thus bestows

The confidence
your love
displays

Searching
my being
in different ways

Only We Matter

Were it not love
we would have thought
bury it deep
set it at naught

This is what we
for years have sought
time for us to
thicken the plot

Sway with the wind
ride with the tide
free up the mind
let feelings glide

Together seek,
respond, reflect
nurture our needs
thus far unmet

In tune with what
we felt for years
now that we know
we have no fears

Discretion

Come to my chamber
for you are no stranger
enter my workplace
kiss me just in case
you feel I deserve it
or you might reserve it
when we are together
not consider whether
this ain't the right place
to hug and to embrace

References

1. Nelson, Dean, 'Fear and Intimidation in Anna Hazare's "Model" Village', *The Telegraph*, 25 August 2011, https://bit.ly/3BIUsn8. Accessed on 8 August 2022.
2. 'Anna and RSS Links Go Back a Long Way: RSS Chief', *Firstpost*, 10 November 2011, https://bit.ly/3Sz2kgL. Accessed on 8 August 2022.
3. 'Secret of fast? Hear it from a Pune doctor', *The Telegraph*, 17 August 2011, https://bit.ly/3zGPogs. Accessed on 8 August 2022.
4. 'Rafale: Yashwant Sinha, Arun Shourie, Prashant Bhushan Call for CBI Probe', *Hindu BusinessLine*, 15 November 2019, https://bit.ly/3vJKNJi. Accessed on 8 August 2022.